WORLD MYTHOLOGIES

# MYTHS OF THE AZTECS

Herald P. McKinley

Cavendish Square
New York

Published in 2016 by Cavendish Square Publishing, LLC
243 5th Avenue, Suite 136, New York, NY 10016



First Edition



CPSIA Compliance Information: Batch #CW16CSQ

All websites were available and accurate when this book was sent to press.

Library of Congress Cataloging-in-Publication Data

McKinley, Herald P..
Myths of the Aztecs / Herald P. McKinley.
pages cm. — (World mythologies)
Includes bibliographical references and index.
ISBN 978-1-5026-0996-0 (hardcover) ISBN 978-1-5026-0997-7 (ebook)
1. Aztecs—Folklore. 2. Aztec mythology—Juvenile literature. I. Title.

F1219.76.F65M35 2016
972—dc23

2015034580

Editorial Director: David McNamara
Editor: Amy Hayes
Copy Editor: Rebecca Rohan
Art Director: Jeffrey Talbot
Designer: Joseph Macri
Senior Production Manager: Jennifer Ryder-Talbot
Production Editor: Renni Johnson
Photo Research: J8 Media

The photographs in this book are used by permission and through the courtesy of: Fototehnik/Shutterstock.com, cover; Dea/A. Gregorio/De Agostini/Getty Images, 4; Felipe Davalos/National Geographic/Getty Images, 8-9; Dea Picture Library/De Agostini/Getty Images, 10, 77; De/G. Dagli Orti/Getty Images, 12, 31, 44; Dea/G. Dagli Orti/De Agostini/Getty Images, 15, 53; Werner Forman/Universal Images Group/Getty Images, 18, 63; Universal History Archive/UIG via Getty Images, 21; Public Domain/http://dl.wdl.org/6725.png/File:Huitzilopochtli, the Principal Aztec God WDL6725.png/Wikimedia Commons, 24-25; Felipe Davalos/National Geographic/Getty Images, 26; Hulton Archive/Getty Images, 35; Werner Forman/Universal Images Group/Getty Images, 37; Museo del Templo Mayor, Mexico City, Mexico/De Agostini Picture Library/G. Dagli Orti/Bridgeman Images, 41; Werner Forman/Universal Images Group/Getty Images, 47; Archives Charmet/Bridgeman Images, 51; North Wind Picture Archives, 59; Public Domain/ http://dl.wdl.org/6749.png/ File:The Eagle, the Snake, and the Cactus in the Founding of Tenochtitlan WDL6749.png/Wikimedia Commons, 69; Ann Ronan Pictures/Print Collector/Getty Images, 72; Spanish School/Private Collection/Bridgeman Images, 80.

Printed in the United States of America

# TABLE OF CONTENTS

INTRODUCTION

# The Importance of Mythology

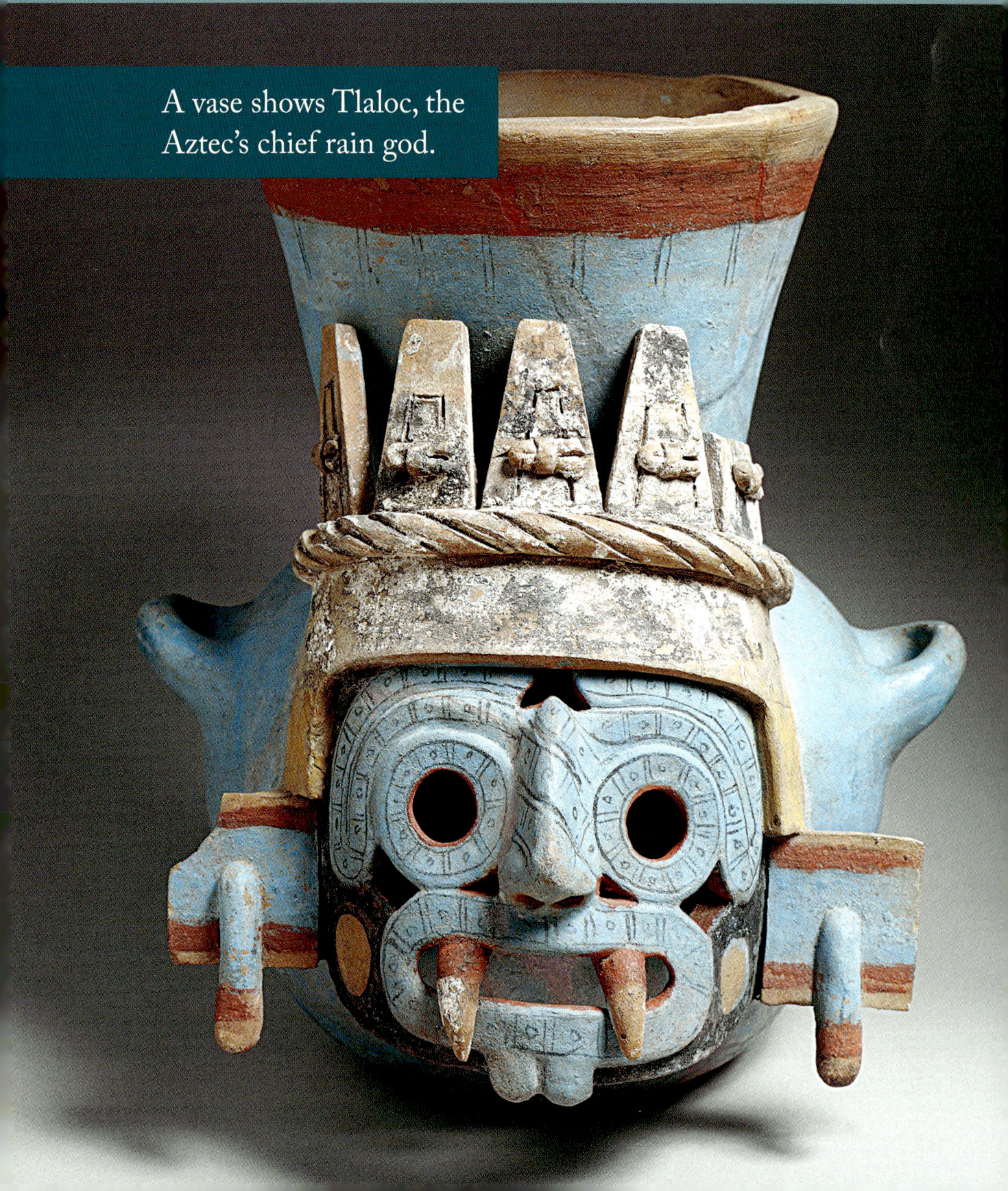

A vase shows Tlaloc, the Aztec's chief rain god.

From folk heroes to gods, campfires to cathedrals, **myths** are stories that are told over and over again. These important stories deepen the identity and customs of a culture. Myths shaped the lives of the people who heard them. These timeless tales of a civilization's gods and heroes were a part of the beliefs, values, and practices of people who lived long ago.

What makes a story a myth? Unlike a narrative written by a particular author, a myth is a traditional story that has been handed down from generation to generation, first orally and later in written form. Nearly all myths tell the deeds of gods, goddesses, and other divine beings. These age-old tales were once widely accepted as true and sacred. Their primary purpose was to explain the mysteries of life and the origins of a society's customs, institutions, and religious rituals.

**Mythology**, the whole collection of myths belonging to a society, played an important role in ancient cultures. In very early times, people created myths to explain the awe-inspiring, uncontrollable forces of nature, such as thunder, lightning, darkness, drought, and death. Even after philosophers and scientists began to develop more rational explanations for these mysteries, myths continued to provide comforting answers to the many questions that could never be fully resolved. People of all cultures have asked the same basic questions about the world around them, such as how did the world begin, what is the purpose of living, and what happens after death?

The myths of the Aztecs are filled with bravery, battles, and blood. There is sacrifice, creation, and destruction. These myths were not just created out of people's imaginations. A civilization's geography, government, and culture all influence what stories are told, and which stories eventually become myth. For example, many myths of the Aztecs include a search for a homeland. The **Mexica** people wandered for many years, and they believed the god **Huitzilopochtli** would bring them to a land that would bring them prosperity and happiness.

Mythology serves as instruction, inspiration, and entertainment. Well-known stories offer people in a society a way to express their fundamental beliefs and values and communicate these beliefs to future generations. Myths preserve and embellish tales of a civilization's accomplishments and teach important lessons about conduct and priorities. These captivating stories provided enjoyment to countless listeners and readers in ancient times, just as they do today.

## A Note on Pronunciations

The names of the Aztec gods and goddesses are hard to spell and even harder to pronounce. The following guidelines may help. When in doubt, do what we do: just say the names any way that makes it easy for you to read and enjoy these wonderful old stories!

**Vowels**

*a* sounds like *ah*

*e* sounds like *ay*

*i* sounds like *ee*

*o* sounds like *oh*

**Consonants**

*c* (before *e* or *i*) sounds like *s*

*c* (before *a* or *o*) sounds like *k*

*cu* sounds like *kw*

*hu* and *uh* sound like *w*

*qu* (before *a*) sounds like *kw*

*qu* (before *e* or *i*) sounds like *k*

When *tl* appears at the end of a word, the *l* is silent.

*x* sounds like *sh*

*z* sounds like *s*

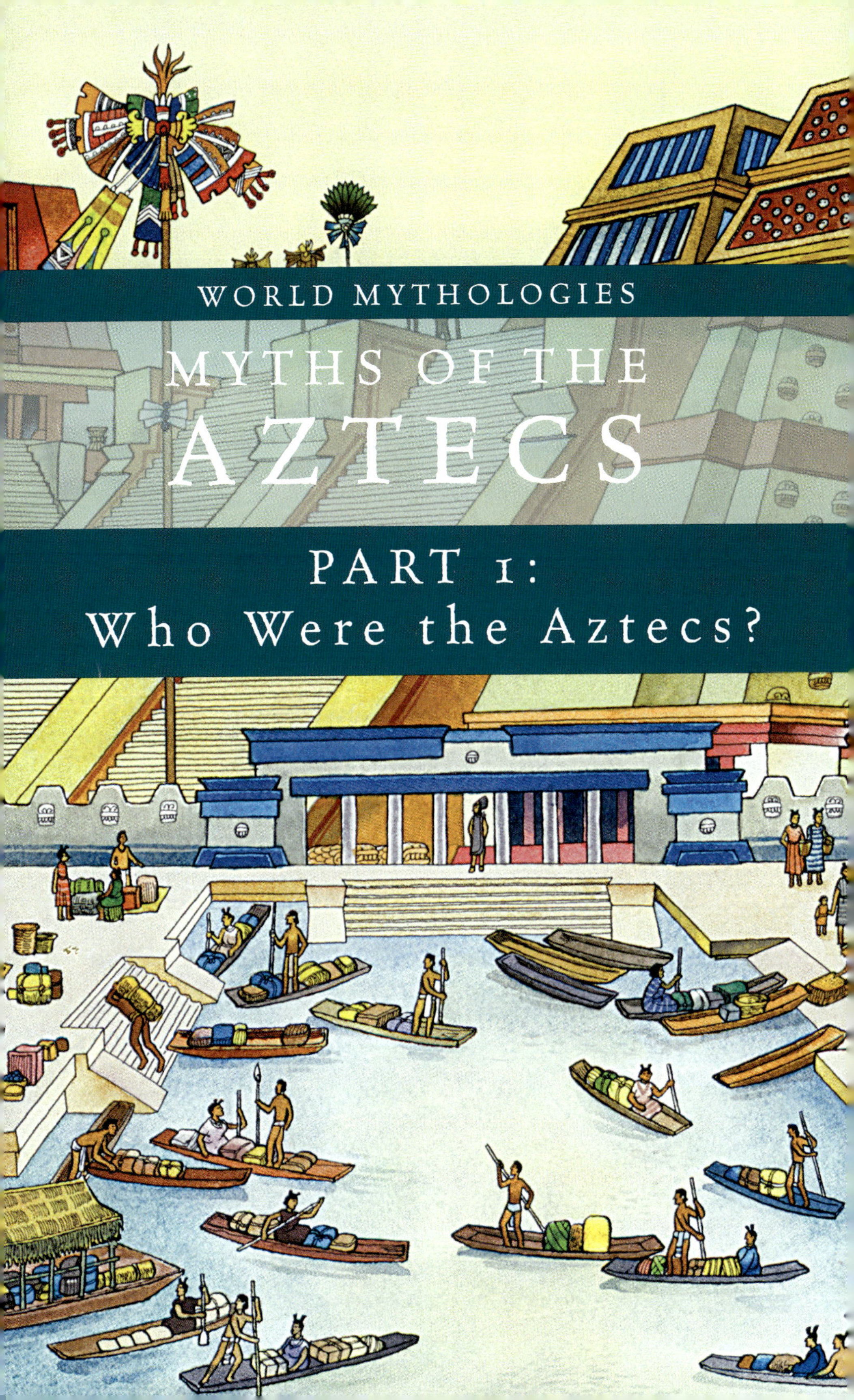

WORLD MYTHOLOGIES

# MYTHS OF THE AZTECS

## PART 1: Who Were the Aztecs?

PART 1: Who Were the Aztecs?

# The Home of the Mexica

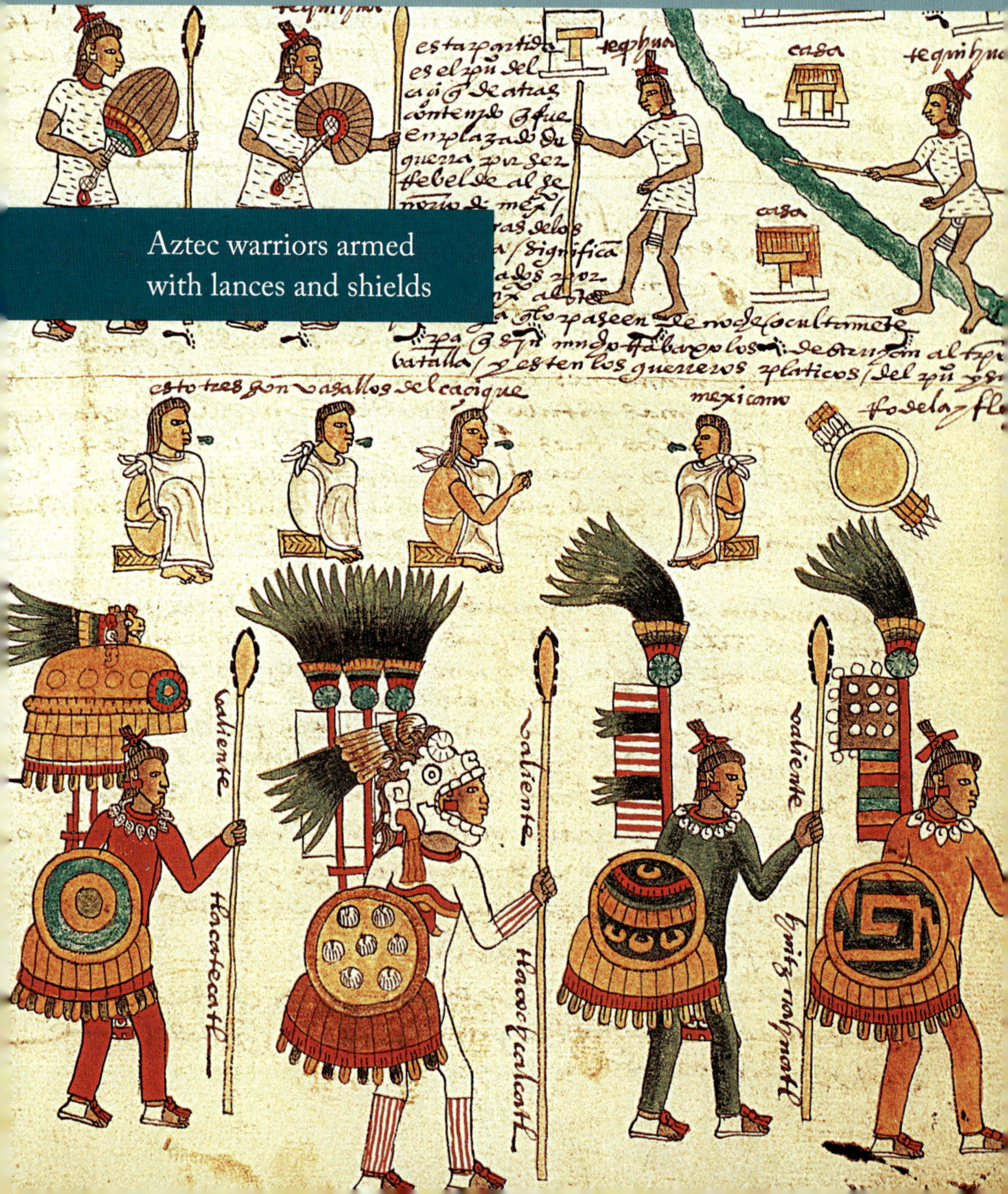


Aztec warriors armed with lances and shields

Long ago, a tribe wandered through the desert, migrating from the north down to an area that is now known as the Valley of Mexico. Eight hundred years ago the tribe, known as the Mexica, found a large plateau surrounded by even higher hills and mountains. Five shallow lakes covered much of this fertile blue-green highland. It was the perfect place for their new home.

The Mexica named their new home **Anahuac**, or in the **Nahuatl** language, "Land between the Waters." Within a few decades, they would transform their tiny village in Anahuac into the center of a mighty empire. Today, we call the people of that empire Aztecs, for Aztlan, their mythical homeland to the north.

The Aztecs lived in a world that was unstable and unpredictable. The Valley of Mexico was ringed by volcanoes that could erupt at any moment, spewing ash, lava, and glowing rocks. Frequent earthquakes shook the ground. The spring rains brought both life-giving waters and devastating floods. Some years, the rains failed, and crops withered in the fields. Thousands of men, women, and children could starve when the harvest was lost to drought or other natural disasters such as locusts or killing frosts.

The stories and cultures of the Aztecs reflected this changeable environment, which was wondrous, but dangerous. "How the Fifth World Came to Be" is a myth that describes how the gods created a series of worlds, then destroyed them with catastrophes including a flood and a rain of fire. This is not unlike the terrors that the Mexica faced in their "Land between the Waters."

# An Aztec Empire

The Aztec capital city of Tenochtitlan means "place of the prickly pear cactus." Construction of this city included strengthening the agricultural land using chinampas.

The Aztecs were the last in a line of great civilizations to emerge from the Valley of Mexico. The Valley had been inhabited by a variety of people, dating back to the Olmecs, an advanced civilization that lived around the twelfth century BCE. Other important **Mesoamerican** civilizations included the Zapotecs, Toltecs, and Maya. Located in Mesoamerica, the Valley of Mexico is a large area of land that today includes the countries of Mexico, Guatemala, Belize, and other parts of Central America.

Wandering groups of Mexica first arrived in the Valley of Mexico around the middle of the thirteenth century CE. By that time, most of the earlier Mesoamerican cultures had declined. A number of small, warring **city-states** inhabited the Land between the Waters. The Mexica roamed from place to place, seeking a home among all these hostile peoples. They finally settled on the shores of wide, shallow Lake Texcoco.

The Mexica proved to be capable farmers. They planted corn and other crops in *chinampas*, narrow strips of farmland created by piling up mud in the shallow lakebeds. They also won acclaim as warriors, fighting in the armies of their stronger neighbors. In 1325, they established their own city on a swampy island in the middle of Lake Texcoco. They named their new capital Tenochtitlán (tay-notch-teet-LAHN), or "Place of the Prickly Pear Cactus."

Over the next century, the Mexica built a strong, disciplined military and expanded their territories. Around 1428, they were powerful enough to form an alliance with two neighboring city-states, Texcoco and

Tlacopan. That Triple Alliance, with the Mexica as the dominant member, forged the mighty Aztec Empire. The fierce Aztec armies conquered a vast realm stretching across Mesoamerica, from the Pacific Ocean to the Gulf of Mexico. The heart of the realm was Tenochtitlán. This magnificent capital became one of the largest and most sophisticated cities in the world, reaching an estimated population between 250,000 and 300,000.

As grand and as mighty as it was, the Aztec Empire lasted less than one hundred years. This was because an invading force had such superior technology that even the most hardened Mexica soldier could not fight against their weapons. This invading force was the Spanish. In 1519, Hernán Cortés sailed to Mexico in search of land and treasure. Cortés and his soldiers formed alliances with the Aztecs' enemies. The Aztecs were no match for Spanish guns. Within two years, the Spaniards and their allies decimated Tenochtitlán. However, Aztec accounts of this overpowering blamed the swift and violent end of their great civilization on mythical forces. "The Aztec World Ends" on page 72 retells that blending of history and religious beliefs.

PART 1: Who Were the Aztecs?

# The Shape of Aztec Society

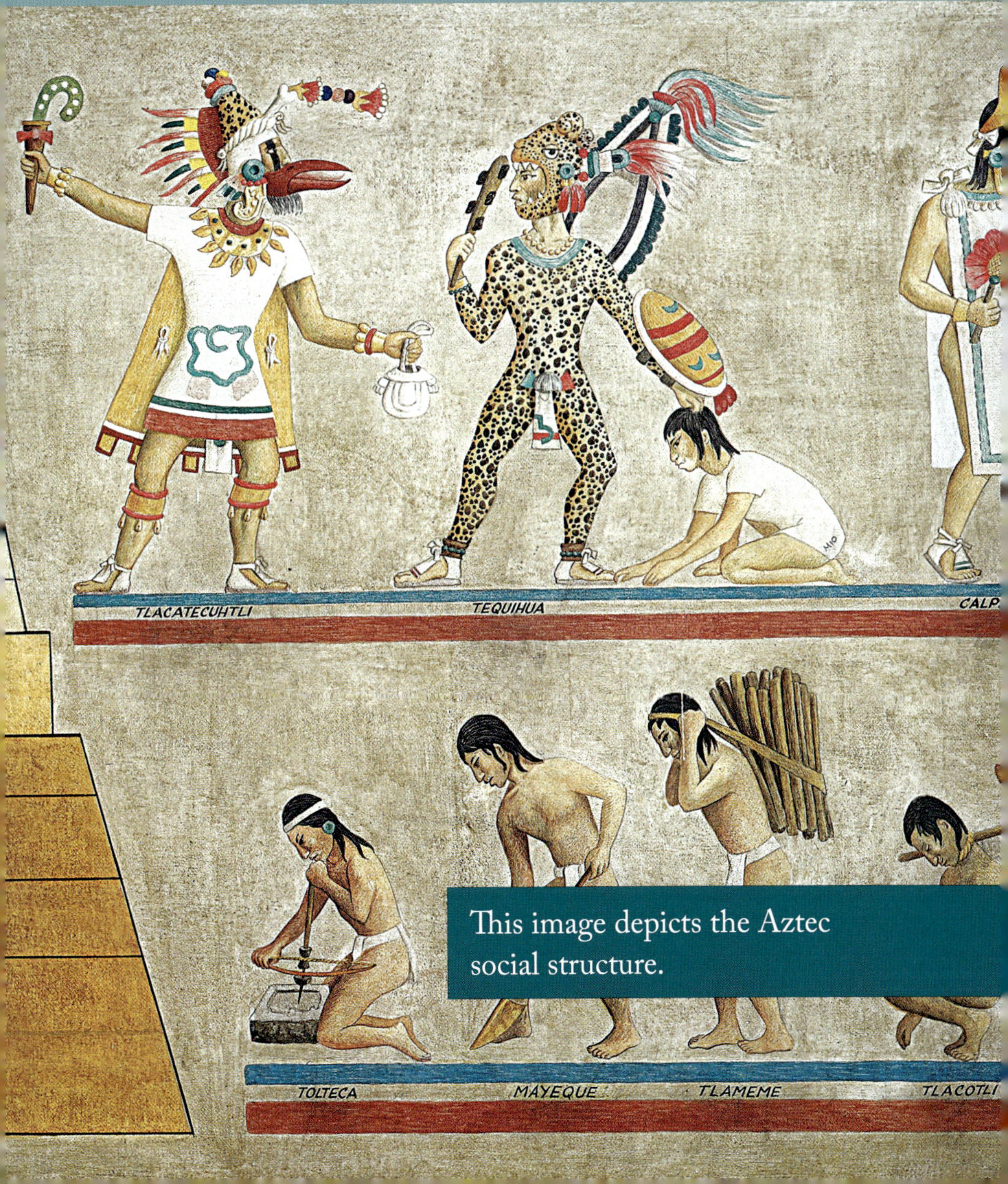


This image depicts the Aztec social structure.

Like many civilizations throughout history and the world, the Aztec society was organized like a pyramid. The few rich and powerful were at the top, while the poorer were vast in number but meager in power.

At the base of this social hierarchy was the body of *macehualtin* (mah-say-WAL-teen), or commoners. These commoners included farmers, fishermen, laborers, craftsmen, and merchants. These hardworking people paid taxes in the form of products. They also were required to labor on public projects such as roads, bridges, and temples and to serve as soldiers in the Aztec army. The children of commoners went to local schools, where they were taught basic occupational skills, the elements of warfare, and good citizenship.

Some macehualtin rose above their fellow commoners to join the narrow middle class. Promising young students were prepared for careers in the priesthood. Brave warriors rose through the military ranks. Gifted painters, goldsmiths, feather workers, and other artisans created luxury goods for the upper classes, while clever sellers became rich city merchants. The most honored merchants were the *pochteca* (poach-TEK-ah), or traders, who traveled to distant lands to bring back coveted goods such as gold and jaguar skins.

At the peak of Aztec society was a small but powerful group of nobles. These highborn individuals included priests, military leaders, and government officials. Nobles had many special privileges, including the right to own land. The wealthiest members of this class lived in great luxury, enjoying the finest homes, food, clothing, and jewels. The children of nobles attended special schools, where priests instructed them in the history and traditions of their elders and the skills of governing.

The noblest of all nobles was the emperor, or *huey tlatoani* (way tlah-toe-AH-nee). The tlatoani was the head of the government, chief priest, and commander in chief of the army. He was responsible for making sure the gods were properly worshipped and for expanding the empire through war. This exalted ruler was elected by a small group of high-ranking nobles, but the Aztecs believed that he was really appointed by the gods.

Aztec society was dominated by men. Women were generally expected to marry and dedicate themselves to their roles as wives and mothers. Although the man was the unquestioned head of the household, wives often enjoyed considerable respect and influence within their own homes. A woman who gave birth was honored as a "valiant warrior." Women also might fight fiercely to defend their homes and families in times of war.

The myths of the Aztecs reflect these highly respected roles. In "The Creation of the Fifth Humans" on page 37, the myth reveres the goddess Cihuacoatl, who helped create the people of the present world. "The Mexica God Huitzilpochtli " on page 53 presents two goddesses who stood for, and watched over, war and sacrifice: Coatlicue and her daughter Coyolxauhqui.

# A Bewildering Variety of Spirits

Tezcatlipoca was the god of the night and darkness.

According to Aztec beliefs, everything that came into existence, from the cry of a newborn infant to the vast ocean, was alive with sacred powers. Many were ethereal, but some became distinctly humanlike in form. These mysterious almost-human spirits were called *teotl* (TAY-aht). However, the term "gods" could also be used.

The list of Aztec gods and goddesses was nearly endless. A few of these divine beings came to Mexico with the Mexica people. Most were adopted from the religions of the Mesoamerican peoples that the Aztecs conquered. A single god might have several different names and functions and might be represented in several forms. Adding to the confusion, the **deities** often overlapped in their areas of responsibility. For example, a number of different teotl were associated with the growing of corn.

Three gods dominated the Aztec religion:

**Tezcatlipoca**, whose name means "Lord of the Smoking Mirror," was all knowing, all powerful, and ever present. He was often associated with the night and darkness. Tezcatlipoca used his magical black mirror to see into the future and search out the secrets in people's hearts.

**Quetzalcoatl**, the "Plumed Serpent," created human beings and gave them many valuable gifts, including agriculture, corn, and the calendar. This beloved god was associated with the morning star, the wind, and priestly wisdom. He was often represented as a serpent covered with the bright green feathers of the **quetzal** bird.

Huitzilopochtli was a fierce god of war and the sun. He led the Mexica people to their island home of Tenochtitlán. His name, which means "Hummingbird on the Left" (or "from the South"), reflects his connection with war and death. The Aztecs believed that hummingbirds were the souls of dead warriors, returning from the paradise of the sun in the South.

Many divine beings were involved with fertility, water, and rain, reflecting the importance of farming in Aztec life. The chief rain god was Tlaloc, or "He Who Makes Things Grow." His sister-wife Chalchiuhtlicue ("She of the Jade Skirt") watched over rivers, lakes, and streams. Another important agricultural deity was Xipe Totec. Like the other Aztec deities, Xipe Totec had several different aspects. As the god of springtime, he watched over seeds, planting, and the growing crops. In his darker forms, he could bring scabs, blindness, and dreadful diseases.

Beyond these teotl, the Aztecs worshipped a huge number of other deities. They worshipped spirits of the trees, mountains, fire, music, dancing, feasting, hunting, gambling, love, beauty, and nearly every other aspect of existence.

# Serving the Gods

An Aztec priest performs a sacrificial offering of a living human's heart.

All Aztec people incorporated religion as part of their daily life. The weather was determined by sacred forces, and so were victories in battle, which were considered the tipping point between order and chaos. The world would survive only if the people did everything possible to secure the blessings of these powerful, unpredictable beings.

Every Aztec home had a small shrine, where the family often gathered to worship the gods and ask for their continued protection. People also performed prayers and rituals as they went about their daily routines. Farmers made offerings to the gods of the rain, sun, earth, and corn. Fishermen appealed to the deities of the waters. Midwives called on the goddesses of birth to watch over women in labor and newborn infants. Everyone took part in the endless round of public festivals that honored the gods through rituals, poetry, plays, music, and dancing.

Priests and priestesses cared for the sacred images of the gods, which were housed in shrines atop pyramid-shaped temples. They also performed sacred ceremonies that helped preserve the balance and order of the universe. These rituals centered around offerings to the gods, which might include gifts of plants, sacrificial animals, gold, or precious gems. The most precious gift of all was human blood.

All worshippers, young and old, offered their blood to the gods by puncturing their earlobes, tongues, and other parts of the body. Priests cut themselves so often that their earlobes became permanently shredded. The Aztecs also sacrificed as many as twenty thousand men, women, and children a year during spectacular religious ceremonies. Most sacrificial victims were prisoners captured in war. Others might be slaves or free individuals chosen for their beauty or other special qualities. Some victims were unwilling participants, while others went proudly to their deaths.

The Aztecs have become infamous throughout history for their tradition of human sacrifice. Where did this tradition begin? The answer may be found in Aztec myths. According to ancient stories, the gods sacrificed their blood to create humans and set the sun moving in the sky. In return for these great gifts, humans were expected to provide the gods with nourishment in the form of human blood. There was a deeper fear beyond gratitude for creation. Without blood sacrifices, the sun might set, only to never come up again. The waters might dry up, and the earth might stop being able to produce crops. With the world dependent on appeasing the gods, blood sacrifices had to be made.

Vitzilopuchtli. Idolo
principal delos Mexica
nos.

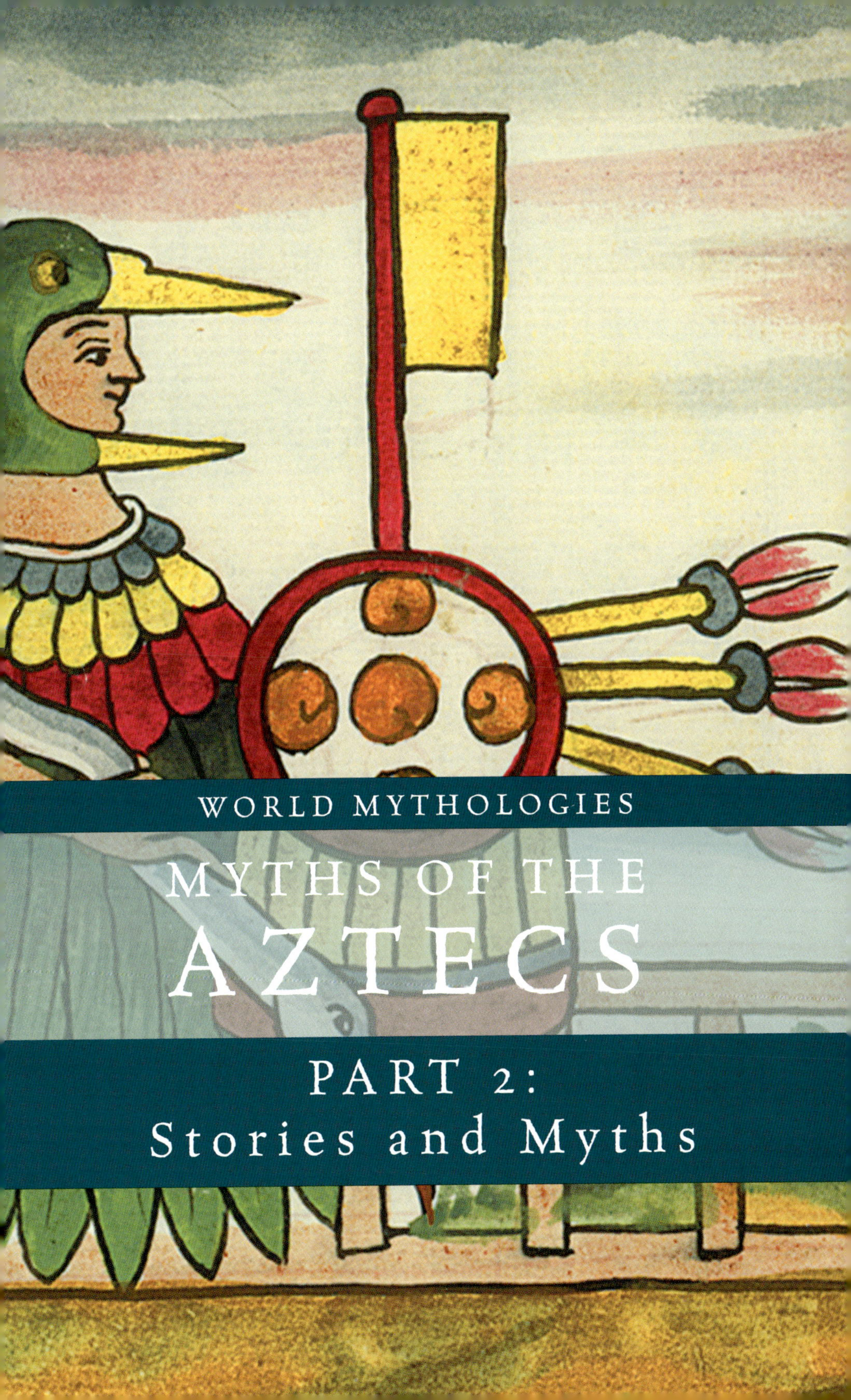

WORLD MYTHOLOGIES

# MYTHS OF THE AZTECS

## PART 2: Stories and Myths

# How the Fifth World Came to Be

Tlaloc's wife, Chalchiuhtlicue, was the Aztec goddess of the waters.

The Aztecs did not believe that they were the first people of the universe. They did not even believe the world they lived in was the first world. Aztec mythology stated that four worlds, or Suns, as the Aztecs called them, existed before the time they lived. Every world was ruled by a different god or goddess. During each Sun, a different race of beings lived on Earth. In time, each world was destroyed, and the inhabitants were either wiped out or transformed into some other form of life. After four of these apocalypses, the gods created the Fifth Sun, the world that the Aztecs knew.

The ancient myth of the Five Suns introduces us to several important Aztec deities. Ometeotl was the source of all existence. This great creator god had a dual (double) nature, combining both male and female forms within one mysterious being. He/she had four sons: Quetzalcoatl, the beloved god associated with the morning star; Tezcatlipoca, who represented the night and darkness; Xipe Totec, god of springtime; and Huitzilopochtli, **patron** god of the Aztecs. Other key players in the creation story include the rain god Tlaloc and his sister-wife Chalchiuhtlicue, goddess of the waters. The conflicts and cooperation among all these deities resulted in both the creation and destruction of the worlds.

The Aztecs recorded their creation story and other myths in texts known as **codices**. The codices were books consisting mainly of pictographs, or word pictures, painted on long, folded scrolls of paper made from bark or deerskin. After the conquest of Mexico, the Spaniards burned most of these sacred texts in an effort to stamp out the Aztec religion. At the same time, a few Spanish missionaries collected and recorded many ancient songs and stories that had been passed down orally for generations. Aztec writers also created new codices about their vanishing traditions. Modern-day scholars have pieced together the Aztec creation myth with the help of these post-conquest texts.

## Dramatis Personae

Dramatis Personae is a Latin phrase meaning "persons of the drama," or cast of characters. Here are the gods who play a role in the creation story of the Aztecs:

**Ometeotl** (oh-may-TAY-oat) Father and mother of the gods

**Xipe Totec** (SHEE-pee TOE-tek) God of new growth and the spring

**Tezcatlipoca** (tez-kaht-lee-PO-kah) God of the night and darkness

**Quetzalcoatl** (ket-sal-KO-wah-tul) God of the morning star

**Huitzilopochtli** (weet-see-lo-POACH-tlee) God of war and the sun; patron god of the Aztecs

**Tlaloc** (TLAH-lok) God of rain

**Chalchiuhtlicue** (chal-chee-oot-LEE-kway) Goddess of lakes, rivers, streams, and mountains

**Tecuciztecatl** (tay-kwah-seez-TAY-kaht) God of snails and the moon

**Nanahuatzin** (nah-nah-WAHT-seen) God of skin diseases

**Tonatiuh** (toe-nah-TEE-wah) God of the sun

## The First Four Worlds

In ancient times there was only one god, whose name was Ometeotl. This mysterious being was both male and female. He was Ometecuhtli, Lord of Duality. She was Omecihuatl, Lady of Duality. He/she dwelt in one body, in a universe bathed in darkness.

Ometeotl gave birth to four children. The oldest was called Xipe Totec. The second and biggest son was Tezcatlipoca. The third brother was Quetzalcoatl. The fourth and smallest brother was Huitzilopochtli.

Together the four brothers created the First Sun. They made the heavens and the earth and the underworld. They made time itself, creating the days and dividing them into months. They created a race of primitive giants, who ate nothing but acorns but were strong enough to pull up trees with their bare hands. The four gods also created Tlaloc and his sister-wife Chalchiuhtlicue, so that the giants would have someone to ask for water. Then Tezcatlipoca turned himself into the sun so that there would be light on the earth.

The First Sun lasted 676 years. Then Quetzalcoatl took a club and knocked his brother out of the sky. The mighty god fell into the sea. When he rose from the water, he was so angry that he turned into a jaguar and devoured all the giants on Earth.

After that, Quetzalcoatl became the sun. He created a new race of people, who had nothing to eat but pine nuts. The Second Sun lasted 364 years. Then Tezcatlipoca took revenge on his brother. He raised a great blast of wind that swept the sun from the sky. The fierce wind blew away all the trees and houses. It carried off all the people, except for a few who were changed into monkeys. You can still see the descendants of the monkey-people swinging through the trees in the forests.

Next, Tlaloc, god of rain, became the sun. The people of this age ate a seed like wheat, which sprouts in the water. The Third Sun lasted 312 years. Then Quetzalcoatl sent a rain of fire. The sun went up in flames, and the trees and houses were consumed by red-hot lava. All the people burned up, except for a few who turned into birds and flew above the molten earth until it cooled and hardened.

Now Tlaloc's wife, Chalchiuhtlicue, became the sun. In this age, the people of the earth lived on a wild seed that was the ancestor of true corn. The Fourth Sun lasted 676 years. Then it rained so long and so hard that the floodwaters rose over the tops of the mountains. All the people were turned into fishes. The sky itself came falling down, washing the sun along with it.

At last, the rains stopped. For fifty-two years the earth lay still, dark, and silent under its blanket of water. Then the four sons of Ometeotl decided to create a space where life could begin again. They made four roads to the center of the earth. They crawled under the edges of the fallen sky, each in a separate quarter. Working together, they raised up the sky-waters.

To keep the sky from falling again, Quetzalcoatl and Tezcatlipoca turned themselves into two enormous trees. The Quetzalcoatl tree glinted with the emerald green feathers of the quetzal bird. The Tezcatlipoca tree glowed with smoky black mirrors. To this day those two mighty trees still support the sky above the earth.

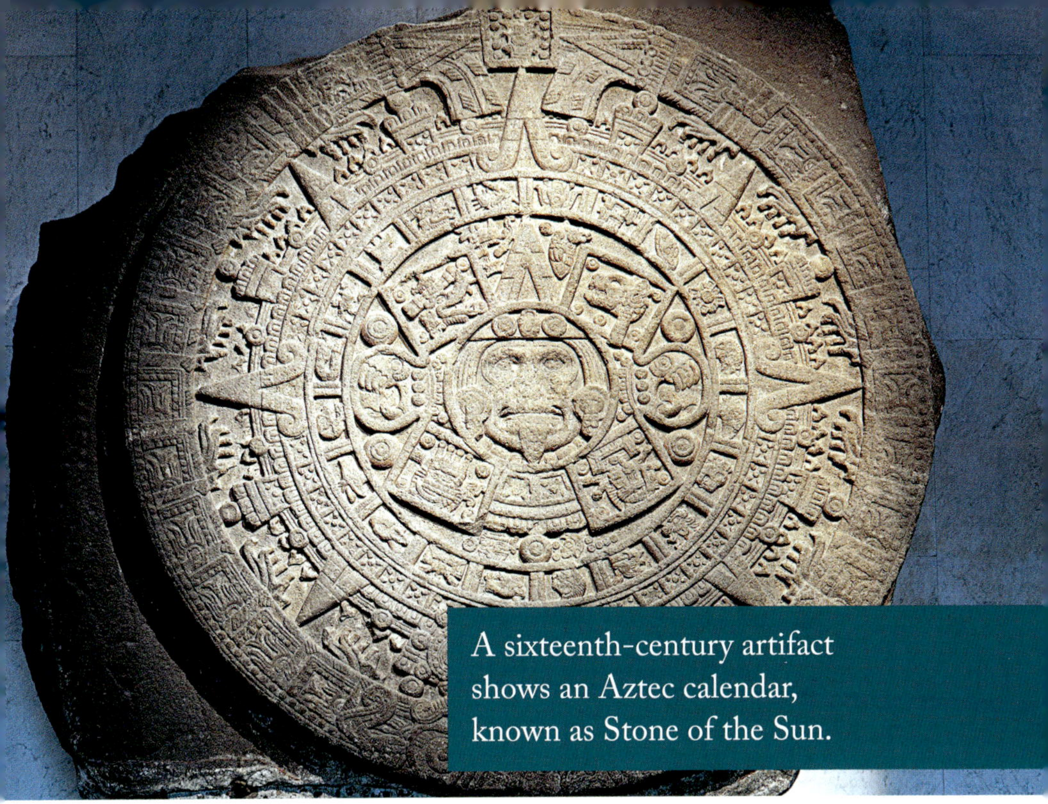

A sixteenth-century artifact shows an Aztec calendar, known as Stone of the Sun.

In appreciation of their great deed, Ometeotl made Quetzalcoatl and Tezcatlipoca masters of the sky and stars. Leaving their trees in place, the two gods walked through the heavens. The white road they traveled on can still be seen in the night sky. Today we call it the Milky Way.

## Creation of the Fifth Sun

After the creation of the fifth world, the gods gathered together in the heavens. "The earth remains in darkness," they said. "Who among us will take it upon himself to become the new sun?"

Tecuciztecatl, the fine and wealthy lord of snails, stepped forward. "O gods, I shall be the one!" he said proudly.

Again the gods spoke. "One is not enough for this important task. Who will be the other one? Who will help bring the dawn?"

This time no one came forward. All the gods were too afraid. They knew that whoever volunteered must sacrifice himself in the fire so that the sun could be born again.

As the gods worried and wondered what to do, Nanahuatzin stood watching. This humble god was small, weak, and misshapen. His skin was covered with ugly sores. He did not dare present himself in the same company as strong, handsome Tecuciztecatl, but when no one else volunteered, the gods turned to him at last. "You! You shall be the one to give light, Nanahuatzin!"

The little god's heart leaped with gladness. "I accept!" he cried quickly. "O gods, you have honored me!"

The two volunteers prepared themselves to celebrate the sacred rituals. For four days, they purified their bodies by fasting. They made offerings on the great fire that the other gods built upon a stone altar. Tecuciztecatl burned fragrant incense and offered gold, gems, and quetzal feathers. Nanahuatzin could offer only reeds, pine needles, and cactus thorns dyed red with his blood. For incense, the humble god burned the scabs picked from his scarred body.

At midnight on the fourth day, the gods adorned the chosen ones for the sacrifice. They dressed Tecuciztecatl in rich garments and crowned him with a tall, feathered headdress. As for poor, humble Nanahuatzin, they dressed him in a loincloth and headdress made of mere paper.

The gods formed two lines, one on each side of the altar. Tecuciztecatl and Nanahuatzin stood between the lines, facing the blazing bonfire. "Take courage, O Tecuciztecatl!" the watching gods shouted. "Cast yourself into the flames!"

## The Earth Monster

According to one version of the Aztec creation story, Quetzalcoatl and Tezcatlipoca worked together to recreate the earth after the destruction of the Fourth Sun. Raw materials for their creation came from the earth goddess Tlaltecuhtli. This monster had hungry mouths all over her body. Quetzalcoatl and Tezcatlipoca captured her, tore her in two, and used the halves to create the sky and the earth. The Aztecs believed that earthquakes were complaints from the mutilated goddess. Only flesh and blood could soothe her hunger and ensure her continued blessings.

The following retelling of this ancient story comes from the *Histoyre du Mechique*, a French translation of a sixteenth-century Spanish text on Aztec mythology.

> [Quetzalcoatl and Tezcatlipoca] changed themselves into two large snakes, of which one seized the goddess from the right hand to the left foot, the other from the left hand to the right foot, and they pulled so much that they broke her in half, and from the half towards the shoulders they made the earth and carried off the other half to heaven. ... After this deed, in order to recompense [repay] the goddess of the earth for the damage that the two gods had done to her, all the gods came down to console her, and ordered that from her would come all the fruit necessary for the life of men; and in order to do this, they made from her hair trees and flowers and grasses, from her skin the very fine grass and small flowers, from her eyes wells and fountains and small caverns, from her mouth rivers and great caverns, from her nose mountain valleys, and from her shoulders mountains. And this goddess sometimes wept at night, desiring to eat men's hearts, and would not be quiet until they were offered to her, nor would she bear fruit unless she was watered with the blood of men.

The proud god took a step forward. He halted. The fire was a raging, terrifying inferno. Once more he advanced. Once more he stopped, struggling to overcome his terror. Finally, Tecuciztecatl turned tail and retreated. He could not jump into the fire.

Now the gods cried out to Nanahuatzin, "Quickly, you! Take heart! O Nanahuatzin, cast yourself into the flames!"

Nanahuatzin closed his eyes. His good heart gave him strength and power. Without hesitation, the little god ran and hurled himself into the center of the fire.

A great tongue of flame licked the heavens. There was a loud crackling and sizzling as the fire devoured Nanahuatzin's body. Beholding the humble god's heroic act, Tecuciztecatl was overcome with shame. With a loud cry, he too leaped into the bonfire.

The sacrifice was complete. Slowly the fire sputtered and died, leaving the world in darkness. The gods sat down and waited for the new sun to rise.

After a long time, a faint light reddened the sky like blood spreading out upon water. The gods looked to the east. Suddenly, Nanahuatzin burst forth. The humble god had been transformed by his sacrifice. Now he was Tonatiuh, the life-giving sun. His shimmering rays warmed the earth, and his light was so dazzling that it was impossible to look into his face.

> Nanahuatzin ... quickly threw and cast himself into the fire.
>
> ~ *Florentine Codex*

But what's this? On the heels of Tonatiuh came Tecuciztecatl, just as big and splendid! When the

A priest offers a human sacrifice atop a Mesoamerican temple pyramid.

gods saw the two suns, they were outraged. How dare Tecuciztecatl shine as brightly as his courageous partner! Just then, a rabbit hopped by. One of the gods reached down and picked up the little animal. He threw the rabbit at the second sun, wounding Tecuciztecatl and dimming his light. Today you can still see the rabbit sprawled across the face of the full moon.

At last, there was one new sun. But something was wrong. Tonatiuh simply hung on the eastern horizon, motionless. "How shall we live?" asked the gods. "How can time progress and the seasons pass if the sun does not move?" At last came the dreadful answer: they all must die in order to give the sun life.

One by one, the gods removed their fine garments. They stood before Quetzalcoatl, and he cut out their hearts with his stone knife. The energy of their lifeblood nourished the sun. At last, Tonatiuh began to follow his appointed path across the sky.

Thanks to the blood of the gods, the sun emerges in the east to battle the darkness every morning. Just as the gods sacrificed themselves to help Tonatiuh move through the sky, so the people give their blood to nourish him on his journey. Every night, the earth swallows the sun. Then the moon comes forth, lending the world his feeble light while his partner travels through the underworld, only to rise again the next morning.

# The Creation of the Fifth Humans

Quetzalcoatl rises from the jaws of the earth, which are represented here in this shell art by a coyote.

After the gods created the world of the Fifth Sun, they created people to populate this new world. Quetzalcoatl took on the great task of recreating humanity. To do this, the wise Quetzalcoatl journeyed to the world of the dead and brought back the bones of the people of the Fourth Sun, who had turned into fish. When the god retrieved the bones, the other gods joined him and used their own blood to bring the bones to life. This created the humans of the world today.

This ancient tale gives us a window into the Aztecs' beliefs about the nature of the universe. According to their traditional tales, the universe consisted of three main regions: the upper world or heavens, the middle world or earthly level, and the underworld. Each of these regions was divided into several levels, which were inhabited by different gods and other supernatural beings. To create the new race of humans, Quetzalcoatl traveled down to the dark and gloomy ninth level of the underworld, known as **Mictlan**. There, he had to outsmart the god of death, who was reluctant to release the bones of the human ancestors.

The story of the creation of humanity also helps explain the Aztecs' view of their role in the universe. Because people had been brought to life through the sacrifice of the gods, they had to give their own blood in return. Human sacrifice not only repaid an ancient debt, but it was also essential to the continuation of life. The world of the Fifth Sun could not continue unless its creators were nourished with the magic essence of life found in human blood.

## Dramatis Personae

**Quetzalcoatl** (ket-sal-KO-wah-tul) God of the morning star

**Mictlantecuhtli** (meek-tlan-tay-KWAH-tlee) God of the dead

**Mictlancihuatl** (meek-tlan-SEE-waht) Goddess of the dead

**Cihuacoatl** (see-wah-KO-waht) Patron goddess of midwives

## Quetzalcoatl Travels to the Underworld

Four ages had come and gone. A new world had been created after the Fourth Sun perished in the great flood. Still the gods were unhappy, because the world had no people to honor and serve them. So they called an assembly. "The earth has been spread out below the sky-waters," they said. "Who will settle there?"

Quetzalcoatl spoke up. "I will journey down to Mictlan," he said. "I will go to the Land of the Dead and bring back the bones of the fish-people. Their bones will become the ancestors of a new race of humans."

So Quetzalcoatl dove down through the body of the earth monster. He journeyed through the first eight layers of the underworld. Through fire and ice, past raging rivers, crashing mountains, and hungry monsters he traveled. At last he reached the ninth and bottom level of the underworld, Mictlan. This desolate realm is home to the spirits of those who died a natural death on Earth. While the souls of dead warriors and other valiant people return to Earth as birds and butterflies, the spirits in Mictlan endure cold winds, dreadful famine, and endless darkness. Mictlan is also the place where the gods store the bones of past generations.

Quetzalcoatl bowed down before the thrones of Mictlantecuhtli and Mictlancihuatl, lord and lady of the dead land. "I have come for the precious bones that you are guarding," he told them.

"What will you do with them?" asked Mictlantecuhtli.

"The gods are sad because there are no people on the earth," answered Quetzalcoatl. "The bones will become the seeds of a new generation."

"Very well," said the crafty god of the dead. "You may take the bones. But first you must prove your worthiness by performing a simple task. You must blow on my conch-shell trumpet as you carry it four times around my sacred realm."

Quetzalcoatl agreed to the dark lord's terms. But when he picked up the trumpet, he saw that it could not make a sound, because it had no holes. Quickly he summoned the worms and asked them to drill holes in the shell. He called for a swarm of bees, which flew inside it. Then the clever god paraded around the underworld, while the bees filled the horn with a loud buzzing sound.

Mictlantecuhtli was displeased, but he could not break his word. "Oh, very well! Take the bones!" he cried.

So Quetzalcoatl gathered up the bones of one man and one woman. He wrapped them in a bundle. Then he hurried off before the lord of Mictlan could change his mind.

A terracotta figure gives shape to Mictlantecuhtli, god of the dead.

Meanwhile, Mictlantecuhtli sat muttering on his throne. Suddenly, he shouted for his servants. "Quick! Quetzalcoatl is taking the precious bones!" he cried. "You must dig a pit to trap him!"

The dark lord's servants hurried on ahead and dug a deep hole. As Quetzalcoatl ran from Mictlan, a flock of quail flew up and startled him. The god stumbled and fell into the pit, whacking his head. His precious bundle split open, and all the bones scattered. As Quetzalcoatl lay unconscious, the quail nibbled the broken bones to many different-sized pieces. (That is the reason people today come in so many different shapes and sizes.)

After a while Quetzalcoatl regained his senses. "What shall I do?" he cried. "Everything has gone wrong. The bones are ruined." Then, a small voice inside the god's head whispered, "However it goes is how it goes. Make the best of it, and complete your journey."

So Quetzalcoatl gathered together all the scattered bits of bones. He carried them up through the nine levels of the underworld, through the earth, to the highest level of the heavens. There he gave them to Cihuacoatl, the ancient goddess who watches over childbirth.

Cihuacoatl put on her sacred eagle-feather headdress. She placed the bones in a bowl and ground them into a fine powder. One by one, all the gods sprinkled drops of their blood over the vessel. Mixing together the powder and the blood, the goddess made a paste. She molded the sticky dough into a man and a woman.

When it was done, the new people of the world breathed in their first breaths. "O gods, the people are born!" spoke Quetzalcoatl. "The people of the Fifth Sun have been given life through your sacrifices!"

## Two Sides of Everything

In "Quetzalcoatl Travels to the Underworld," the god travels to the Land of the Dead in order to restore life to the world. To the Aztecs, that journey would have made perfect sense. According to their beliefs, life and death were simply two sides of the same reality. So were male and female, darkness and light, weakness and strength, creation and destruction. Everything in the world had two natures, which were both opposite and complementary (meaning that the two halves together made a whole).

A poem recited by modern-day descendants of the Aztecs in the Mexican state of Puebla may help us understand these age-old beliefs. The poet is reflecting on the complex connections between life and death. Humans must eat in order to live, but eating requires killing plants and animals, the "fruits of the earth." In this way, life is born of death. The poem also reminds us that one day we will all return to the same earth that gave us life.

We live here on this earth
We are all fruits of the earth
the earth sustains us
we grow her, on the earth and lower
and when we die we wither in the earth
we are all fruits of the earth
We eat of the earth
because the earth eats us.

PART 2: Stories and Myths

# The Gifts of the Gods

A long gourd extracts the sap of the maguey plant, used to make pulque.

The gods had created a new world and a new people to live in it. However, now they had to provide sustenance for the people to eat. The most important gift the gods gave to their new creations was **maize**, or corn. Maize was the central crop of early Mesoamerica. Nobles and commoners alike ate a diet based on maize prepared in various forms, such as soups, tortillas, and tamales. According to the religious tales, it was Quetzalcoatl who brought this vital food to the Aztec people.

Quetzalcoatl also gave humankind many other valuable gifts. Aztec myths credit him with introducing the calendar, establishing the priesthood, instructing people in the arts of weaving and stonework, and other acts to ensure humanity's survival. In addition, the beloved god helped give the Aztecs a gift that added pleasure to life: **pulque**.

Pulque (pronounced POOL-kay) is an alcoholic beverage made from the sap of the maguey plant. This sacred drink was believed to have magical properties that gave people strength and allowed them to experience other levels of reality. The Aztecs used pulque mainly in religious rituals. Nobles, warriors, nursing mothers, the elderly, and the sick were also permitted to sample it on occasion. Public drunkenness was strongly condemned and strictly punished, however. After the third offense, a person who was too fond of the potent powers of pulque could be put to death.

## Dramatis Personae

**Quetzalcoatl** (ket-sal-KO-wah-tul) God of the morning star

**Nanahuatl** (nah-NAH-waht) God of lightning

**Tlaloc** (TLAH-lok) God of rain

**Mayahuel** (may-AH-well) Goddess of the maguey plant

**Tzitzimitl** (tzee-TZEE-meet) Queen of the star demons

## Quetzalcoatl and the Corn

What shall they eat?" The gods looked at one another and pondered the question. How would the new race of humans, the people of the Fifth Sun, find nourishment in a world washed clean of vegetation?

As so often happens, it was Quetzalcoatl who found the answer. Peering down from the heavens, the wise god saw a small red ant carrying a kernel of corn. Quetzalcoatl hurried down to the earth. "Where did you get that?" he asked the ant. "Tell me where you found that wonderful food."

At first, the ant refused to answer. It was afraid that the god would take away all its precious corn. But Quetzalcoatl was persistent, and when a mighty god demands an answer, a humble ant cannot long resist him. "Very well, I will show you the source of the corn," the ant said finally. "But you are much too big to enter the secret passageways where it lies hidden."

Instantly Quetzalcoatl changed himself into a little black ant. He followed the red ant over the hills and valleys of Anahuac, all the way to Food Mountain. The god saw hundreds of ants disappearing through a crack in the rock. Joining the line, he entered a long, narrow tunnel. He scurried down the passage to the center of the mountain. There he found a chamber filled with corn in four colors: white, black, red, and yellow. He also saw piles of beans, squash seeds, pepper seeds, and many other seeds and grains that the ants had hidden away when the world of the Fourth Sun was drowned in the great flood.

Quetzalcoatl became a god associated with vegetation and fertility. Here he carries maize cobs on his back.

Quetzalcoatl picked up a kernel of corn with his strong jaws. He labored back up the tunnel and lay down his burden. Down he went again, into the heart of the mountain. Back he came, with another kernel. Finally, the little black ant had gathered up a tidy mound of corn. Snap! He transformed himself back into a god. Then Quetzalcoatl carried the corn up to the heavens, where the other gods were waiting.

The gods tasted the corn. It was delicious! They chewed it up and placed the mash in the mouths of human infants. The hungry babies grew big and strong on the wholesome meal.

"Corn is the perfect food to strengthen and nourish the humans!" the gods declared. "But how will we get all of it out of Food Mountain?"

Again, Quetzalcoatl thought that he had the answer. He wrapped a huge rope around Food Mountain and tried to pull it from the earth. The god strained and struggled, but even with his great powers, the gigantic rock would not budge.

Nanahuatl, god of lightning, stepped forward. "I will crack it open," he declared, and he hurled his fiery weapon. There was a blinding flash as the lightning struck Food Mountain, splitting it wide open. All the gods cheered as the food came pouring out of the heart of the mountain.

But even as they celebrated, there arose a great commotion. Tlaloc, the god of rain who dwells on the mountaintops, was angered by the destruction of Food Mountain. Together with his four children, the rain gods of the four directions, he descended on the shattered pile of rocks. The swirling mass of gods snatched up all the corn kernels. They stole the beans and all the seeds and grains. Then they swept back to their hiding places high up in the mountains.

So it was that Quetzalcoatl found corn and other good things to nourish the people of the Fifth Sun. But the lords of rain still guard the food that was hidden in the mountain. Each year they give some of it back to humankind—some years more, other years less. That is why the people offer prayers and sacrifices to Tlaloc, asking him to send just the right amount of rain to make the crops grow in abundance.

## Rain Prayer

The Aztecs worshipped a host of gods and goddesses associated with maize and other crops. Through rituals celebrated at various times throughout the growing season, they honored these deities and asked for their blessings. The following verses come from a long prayer to Tlaloc, god of rain. The prayer was recited as part of a special ceremony performed in times of drought.

Oh, the fruits of the earth lie panting;
the sister of the gods, the sustenances of life,
feebly drags herself along,
she is covered with dust, she is covered with cobwebs,
she is utterly worn and weary.

And behold, the people, the subjects, are perishing!
Their eyelids are puffy, their mouths dry as straw,
their bones are dessicated [dried up], and they are twisted and gaunt,
their lips are thin, their necks pale and scrawny ...

O Lord, Beloved Lord, O Provider!
May it be in your heart to grant, to give, to bring comfort to the earth
and all that lives from it, all that grows on it.
And you who inhabit the four quarters of the universe,
you the Lords of Verdure [greenness], you the Providers,
you the Lords of the Mountain Heights, you the Lords of the
    Cavernous Depths,
I call out, I cry out to you:
come, bring yourselves here,
comfort the people, slake the thirst of the earth;
the earth and the animals, the leaves and stalks
are watching and waiting and crying out.
O gods, Our Lords, make haste!

## The Happiness of Pulque

Corn and beans fill the belly, but they cannot gladden the heart. Although the people of the Fifth Sun had everything they needed to survive, still they seemed unhappy. "We must find a way to give the humans joy," the gods said to one another. "Only then will they sing and dance and praise those who created them."

Quetzalcoatl floated on the wind, searching for an answer to the problem. What brings laughter and happiness? he wondered. Gradually his thoughts turned to the goddess Mayahuel. Long had he dreamed of that maiden's sweet innocence and enchanting beauty. But Mayahuel dwelt in the sky, in a house fiercely guarded by her ancient grandmother Tzitzimitl, and Tzitzimitl was queen of the **tzitzimime**, the dreadful star demons who attack the sun each dawn, hoping to devour it completely.

Ha! Quetzalcoatl resolved to brave the wrath of Tzitzimitl! In a flash he soared to the sky-home of the tzitzimime. He found Mayahuel and her grandmother sleeping. Gently, he awakened the lovely young maiden. "I have come to get you," he whispered. "Will you come with me down to the world of humans?"

The moment Mayahuel saw the god's handsome face, she consented. Quetzalcoatl lifted her upon his shoulders, and together they descended to the earth. When they touched the ground, the lovers entwined. They transformed themselves into a beautiful tree to hide from Tzitzimitl. The great tree had two branches, one belonging to Quetzalcoatl, the other to Mayahuel.

Soon Tzitzimitl awakened and saw that her granddaughter had left her. With her magic, she knew at

The goddess Mayahuel wears a headdress of green feathers and a triangular cape.

once what had happened. Screaming in rage, the ancient goddess summoned the tzitzimime. Then she swooped down to the earth with her dreadful servants to search for her disobedient granddaughter.

The demons soared over the fields, lakes, and mountains. When they came to the great tree, the two branches shuddered. Tzitzimitl peered at the tree suspiciously. Suddenly, she recognized her granddaughter from a single white blossom on one of the branches. In a fit of fury, the old hag tore the branch from the tree. She shredded it to bits with her teeth and claws. She handed some of the pieces to her companions,

> As soon as they arrived on earth, they transformed themselves into a tree.
>
> ~ *Histoyre du Mechique*

who devoured them greedily. Then, as quickly as they had come, the demons flew back up to their home in the sky.

Now the branch of Quetzalcoatl stood alone on the broken tree. As soon as the tzitzimime were gone, the god changed back to his rightful form. Sadly, he surveyed the broken bits of Mayahuel left behind by the ravenous demons. Then he tenderly gathered up the goddess's remains and buried them in the earth.

The sun shined. The rains fell. Tender green shoots pushed up from the ground where Mayahuel lay buried. In time, the plant grew tall and strong. It grew into the first maguey!

The people of the earth soon discovered that the wonderful new plant was nearly as useful as corn. They used its fibers for weaving cloth and making rope, its thorns for needles, its leaves for paper and roofing. Its sweet white sap had healing powers. Best of all, when the sap of the maguey was left to ferment, it made a drink with magical powers.

The drink, the sacred pulque, was certainly special, for those who drank it felt a surge of joy in their hearts. It made them want to sing and dance and laugh out loud. The people of the world wanted to celebrate the gods who created them. In pulque, the Aztecs at last knew happiness.

PART 2: Stories and Myths

# The Mexica God Huitzilopochtli

This Aztec statue depicts the goddess Coatlicue, mother of Huitzilopochtli.

Like the Romans, the Aztecs adopted most of their gods from the other civilizations. The Mexica people worshiped gods that originated from a patchwork of earlier peoples of Mesoamerica. However, one major exception was the fierce war god Huitzilopochtli. The people who eventually became the Aztecs brought this god with them when they migrated down from the north.

As the Aztecs rose in power, so did the importance of their tribal god. As time went on, Huitzilopochtli assumed some of the roles associated with even earlier gods. In some myths, for example, he replaced Nanahuatzin as the god who emerged as the Fifth Sun.

According to mythology, Huitzilopochtli was an invincible warrior from the moment of his birth. While he was still in the womb, he learned that his jealous sister, the moon goddess Coyolxauhqui, planned to kill him and his mother. Bursting forth from his mother's body, he defeated his sister and her army of four hundred gods. (To the Aztecs, four hundred meant a number too great to be counted.) Then the infant god beheaded Coyolxauhqui and hurled her body down the side of a mountain.

Modern-day scholars believe that this gory story may represent the constant struggle between light and darkness. The newly born Huitzilopochtli conquered his sister and her army just as the rising sun triumphs over the moon and stars each morning. To ensure the sun's continued victory, the Aztecs waged an endless series of wars. Prisoners of war were often sacrificed in Huitzilopochtli's shrine atop the Great Temple pyramid in Tenochtitlán.

The victims' blood and hearts were offered to the god, to nourish him for his daily battle against the forces of darkness. Then the lifeless bodies were rolled down the steps onto a huge circular image of Coyolxauhqui, repeating Huitzilopochtli's victory over his sister.

## Dramatis Personae

**Coatlicue** (ko-waht-LEE-kway) Goddess of agriculture; mother of Huitzilopochtli

**Mixcoatl** (meesh-KO-waht) God of hunting

**Coyolxauhqui** (koy-yol-SHAOW-kee) Goddess of fire and the moon

**Cuahuitlicac** (kwah-wee-TLEE-kak) One of the Four Hundred Southerners

**Huitzilopochtli** (weet-see-lo-POACH-tlee) God of war and the sun; patron god of the Aztecs

## The Birth of Huitzilopochtli

On the slopes of Coatepec, the Serpent Mountain, dwelt a woman named Coatlicue. This virtuous woman was the wife of Mixcoatl, god of hunting. She had borne her husband one daughter, Coyolxauhqui, and a multitude of gods known as the Four Hundred Southerners. After giving birth to all these children, Coatlicue had taken a vow of chastity. She would spend the remainder of her days as a priestess, doing holy work in the shrine at the top of the sacred mountain.

One day Coatlicue was sweeping out the shrine when a ball of brightly colored feathers came drifting down from the sky. The woman picked up the feathers and tucked them in the waistband of her skirt. After she had finished sweeping, she looked for them. They had vanished! Coatlicue did not know it, but the feathered ball had magical powers. From that moment, she was with child.

Soon, Coyolxauhqui and the Four Hundred Southerners noticed their mother's belly beginning to swell. Their father, Mixcoatl, had been away for many months, so he could not have caused the pregnancy. There was only one possible explanation: Coatlicue must have broken her vow of chastity. Through her sinful act, she had insulted her husband and dishonored the entire family.

"Who has done this to you?" the gods asked their mother. "Who has made you pregnant?" When the poor woman could not answer, they became even more outraged.

"Brothers, our mother's sins have brought disgrace on our family," said Coyolxauhqui. "Why does she not reveal the name of her lover, so that we can punish him? There is only one way to deal with such wickedness. We must kill her!"

These bitter words fanned the anger of the gods into a raging fury. Together the Four Hundred Southerners vowed to join their sister in destroying their mother. First, they had to prepare for battle. They wound their hair around their heads in the style of warriors. They put on their thick armor and decorated it with streamers of colored paper. They tied war bells around the calves of their legs. Then they gathered up their bows and their sharp barbed arrows.

As the warriors were making their preparations, one slipped away from camp. Forgetting his vow to his sister and brothers, Cuahuitlicac made his way to Serpent Mountain. He found his mother in the shrine at the top and told her about the plot against her.

When Coatlicue learned of her children's cruel plan, she began to tremble with fear. Suddenly, she heard her unborn child speaking from her womb. "Do not be afraid," said the voice of Huitzilopochtli. "I know what I must do." Those confident words comforted the poor woman, so that at once her heart was peaceful and quiet.

The following morning, the Four Hundred Southerners moved out, with Coyolxauhqui guiding them. The mighty war party marched across the country, row after row, in an orderly formation. After a journey of several days, the warriors reached the foot of Serpent Mountain. Once again Cuahuitlicac sneaked off and ran ahead to warn his mother of their progress. "My brothers are climbing up the side of the mountain," he told her. "Now they have reached the top. They are drawing near. Here they are, with Coyolxauhqui leading them!"

At that very moment, Huitzilopochtli was born. The magnificent god sprang from his mother's womb fully armed and ready for battle. His arms and legs were painted blue. On his head was his blue-green headdress of hummingbird feathers. In his hands were his spears and his magical shield of eagle feathers. Most fearsome of all was his terrible spear-thrower, made from a living serpent. At a word from the god, the fire-serpent burst into flames that burned as bright as lightning.

Huitzilopochtli lashed out with his lightning bolt. With one deadly stroke, he sliced Coyolxauhqui's head from her shoulders. He tossed the head into the sky, where it was born again as the moon. He hurled his sister's body down the mountainside. As it fell, it broke into pieces, so that her arms and legs landed in different places.

> Her hands, her legs, her body fell in different places.
>
> ~ *Florentine Codex*

Then the god turned his divine anger against his half brothers, the Four Hundred Southerners. He drove them off the mountaintop, and as they fled, he pursued them like a hunter chasing rabbits. In vain, the warriors tried to rally against him. In vain, they clashed their shields and rattled their bells, hoping to frighten him. They could do nothing to turn aside the fierce and fearless warrior.

Four times, Huitzilopochtli made his brothers run around the base of the mountain, until they stumbled and begged for mercy. A very few managed to escape back to the south. The wrathful god caught all the others. Finally, Huitzilopochtli struck them with his fire-serpent and completely obliterated them.

Every day this divine combat plays out across the sky. Each dawn, the sun rises, newborn from the body of the earth. Each morning, Huitzilopochtli fights the moon and scatters the unnumbered stars across the night sky.

PART 2: Stories and Myths

# Finding Their True Home

A hand-colored woodcut shows Tenochtitlán, the island capital of Aztec Mexico.

There were a few originally Mexica myths that Aztecs liked to tell. Like their gods, the myths of the Aztecs were largely adopted and passed down from earlier peoples of Mesoamerica. Yet, the Aztecs did have important myths that dealt with their history. Many of these historical tales related to the beginnings of the Mexica people. The tales of the migration to Tenochtitlán, the swampy island that would become the heart of their empire, are some of the most revered and important original myths.

The Aztecs told many different versions of their migration myth. According to the best-known account, the Mexica once lived in a mysterious place far to the north known as Aztlan, or "Place of Herons." One day, Huitzilopochtli commanded them to journey south to a distant land where he would make them the rulers of a mighty nation. With the god leading the way, the people set out on their long, difficult migration. After many years, they reached the shores of Lake Texcoco in the Valley of Mexico. There they saw a huge eagle perched on a cactus, a sign that they had reached the "promised land."

The Aztec migration story interweaves history and mythology. Some of the places described in the story are imaginary, while others were real towns and cities in early Mesoamerica. Some of the episodes echo the ancient stories of other peoples, while others are probably based on historical events. To the Aztecs, this creative retelling of history was sacred and true. Children studied the migration story in school, poets recited it in verses, and artists recorded it in codices. Passed down through all these different avenues, the tale of their ancestors' rise to glory was a source of pride from generation to generation. Most importantly, the Aztecs regarded the heroic story as proof that it was their divine destiny to rule over all the conquered peoples of Mesoamerica.

## Dramatis Personae

**Huitzilopochtli** (weet-see-lo-POACH-tlee) God of war and the sun; patron god of the Aztecs

**Malinalxochitl** (mah-lee-nahl-SHOW-cheet) Evil sorceress; sister of Huitzilopochtli

**Copil** (KO-peel) Evil sorcerer; son of Malinalxochitl

**Achitometl** (ah-chee-TOE-mate) King of the ancient city of Culhuacan

## A Sacred Dream

In the distant past, in the days of the grandfathers of the grandfathers, the Mexica people lived far to the north in Aztlan. This ancient city on a lake was a wonderful place. The waters abounded with fish and birds, and the fields produced rich harvests of corn. The people were never sad or hungry, and they never grew old. When they became weary, they simply climbed a tall mountain in the center of Aztlan. The higher they climbed, the younger they became. When they reached the age they desired, they rested awhile and then came down from the mountain.

The Mexica shared their blessed homeland with six other tribes. One by one, the people of those tribes grew restless and left Aztlan. Finally, there was no one left but the Mexica. For more than three hundred years, they dwelt in the northern paradise alone.

One night, Huitzilopochtli appeared to one of his priests in a dream. "In the south, there is an island in the middle of blue waters," the great god whispered. "On the island grows a tall cactus. On the cactus stands an eagle, basking in the rays of the sun. In his talons, the eagle holds a small, precious bird. There, in your new home, your destiny awaits you. There, you will become the mightiest of all nations."

The Mexica were overjoyed when they learned of the god's message. Quickly, they prepared to leave their homeland. Four priests would serve as leaders during the journey. The priests would carry the sacred image of Huitzilopochtli on their backs. The god would speak to them, and they would relay his pronouncements to the rest of the travelers. In this way, Huitzilopochtli would guide his chosen people across the wilderness to the place of destiny.

## The Travels and Towns

For many generations, the Mexica wandered through strange lands. They endured hunger and thirst, plagues and tempests, locusts and hailstorms. Scorned by the inhabitants of the lands through which they passed, they fought many small skirmishes and larger battles. From time to time, the wanderers stopped to rest in fertile places. At each stop, they erected a temple to Huitzilopochtli. They built homes and planted maize and other crops to sustain them. After a while—sometimes ten years, sometimes as long as twenty—their god would

A destructive and angry sorceress goddess, shown here in artwork depicting the four stages of a woman's life, founded the town of Malinalco after being left behind by the Mexica.

command them to move on, and they would obey him. Often they left behind the old, sick, and weary when they resumed their journey. In this way, the Mexica founded many towns and populated many places during their long migration.

After a number of years, the travelers came to a place called Patzcuaro, where they found a clear lake filled with all kinds of fish. The priests asked Huitzilopochtli if they could leave part of their group in this pleasant land. The god granted their request and told them how to accomplish it. The next day, as some of the men and women were bathing in the lake, others sneaked up and stole their cloaks, skirts, and blouses. When the bathers came out of the water, they could not find their clothes. They hurried back to camp and saw that it was abandoned. Naked and forsaken, they decided to remain in Patzcuaro. That is why the people of that land used to walk about with their private parts uncovered.

The Mexica traveled on to the town now known as Malinalco. There they abandoned the sorceress Malinalxochitl, who was a sister of Huitzilopochtli. Malinalxochitl was very beautiful but also very cruel. She was so skilled in magic that she could command deadly snakes, scorpions, and spiders to kill anyone who angered her. The priests had begged Huitzilopochtli to rid them of this evil woman. The god had told them to abandon Malinalxochitl while she lay sleeping. When the woman awakened and saw that she had been tricked, she wept in anger. Cursing her brother's name, she settled in the town that bears her name. To this day, her descendants in Malinalco have the reputation of being sorcerers.

Next, the Mexica stopped in Coatepec, the land of Huitzilopochtli's birth. There, they built a dam across a river. The waters overflowed, flooding the plains. Soon reeds, rushes, willows, and cypresses crowded the banks of the lake they had created. Fish multiplied in the waters, attracting many different kinds of water birds. "O great Huitzilopochtli, this is surely the land that you promised," the people sang happily. "This will be the capital of your kingdom."

Huitzilopochtli became enraged when he heard their foolish singing. "Are you greater than I? Do you dare give opinions on those things that I have determined?" he thundered. In his fury the god punched a hole in the dam, and the waters poured out. All the plants and trees withered. All the fish perished, and the birds flew away.

Frightened and humbled, the Mexica continued on their journey. After many more years of wandering, they came to Chapultepec, on the shores of Lake Texcoco. Then Huitzilopochtli spoke to the people, warning them to take courage. The Promised Land was near, but before they reached it, they would face fierce opposition from a new enemy. Malinalxochitl, the evil woman abandoned earlier in their travels, had borne a son named Copil. The sorceress had raised this terrible youth to despise his uncle. She had taught him all her tricks and witchcraft. Now, Copil was coming with a gigantic army to take vengeance on Huitzilopochtli and his followers.

Quickly, the Mexica prepared their spears and arrows. When Copil's army attacked, they fought back courageously. They were greatly outnumbered, but somehow they managed to hack their way through the enemy ranks to safety.

Meanwhile, Huitzilopochtli chased after Copil and killed him. The god slashed open his nephew's chest and tore out his heart. He gave this to his chief priest, instructing the man to cast it out over Lake Texcoco. The heart of the slain sorcerer fell on a rock on an island in the middle of the lake. The place where it landed would become the heart of the Aztec Empire.

## A Prophecy Fulfilled

Copil had been defeated, but the Mexica people were weary and discouraged. Surrounded by enemies, they turned once again to Huitzilopochtli. "Be of strong heart!" their god told them. "Send envoys to Achitometl, king of Culhuacan. Ask him to give you a place in his country to settle."

So the people sent messengers to the great city of Culhuacan. Huitzilopochtli softened the king's heart, and Achitometl ordered his chieftains to give the Mexica whatever they requested. But the chiefs wanted only to be rid of the ragged band of wanderers. They debated how to manage that while still obeying the king's orders. Finally, they told the Mexica that they could settle in Tizapan, a barren wasteland infested with poisonous snakes and lizards.

The Mexica had no choice but to accept the offer. When they reached Tizapan and saw all the deadly reptiles, they were horrified. Again, Huitzilopochtli spoke to the priests. He told them how to catch the snakes and lizards and eat them. Soon, the people became so fond of boiled and roasted reptiles that they consumed nearly all of them. In fact, they were so contented in their new home that they never wished to leave it. That did not please Huitzilopochtli. He had led his people through

## Travelers in New Lands

According to the Aztecs' sacred history, their ancestors endured many hardships during their long journey to the Promised Land. Often their troubles came at the hands of earlier migrants who had reached Mexico before them. This ancient song tells the story of the Aztecs' rejection by the people they would one day conquer.

As they came,
as they went along their road,
they were no longer received anywhere,
they were rejected everywhere,
no one knew their face.
Everywhere they were asked:
"Who are you?
From where do you come?"
Thus nowhere could they settle,
they were always thrown out,
everywhere were they persecuted.
They passed through Coatepec,
they passed through Tollan [Tula] ...
Next, to Chapultepec
where many peoples came to settle ...
Mexico did not yet exist,
there still were fields of bulrushes and reeds
where now is Mexico.

the wilderness to found a mighty nation. He intended to make them lords over all the nations, not over snakes and lizards. So the great god devised a plan to put an end to the peace and quiet.

A time came when Achitometl sent his chiefs to see how the people of Tizapan were faring. The king's men expected to find the wretched settlers nearly wiped out by the poisonous reptiles. Instead, they saw a splendid temple, neatly cultivated fields, and snakes boiling in cook pots. When they returned with their report, the king was amazed and a little frightened by the remarkable strangers. He quickly granted the Mexica's one request: that he send his beloved daughter to become the bride of their god Huitzilopochtli.

When the princess arrived in Tizapan, the Mexica did as their god had commanded them. They placed her on an altar and sacrificed her. After the girl was dead, they removed her skin. They draped it over a young priest as a sacred costume. Then they invited the king of Culhuacan to come to a festival honoring their new goddess.

King Achitometl accepted the invitation. Bearing offerings of fine food, flowers, and incense, he and his nobles traveled to Tizapan. There, they were greeted as honored guests. They rested, and they dined. Then, the Mexica invited the king to worship in the temple.

Achitometl entered the inner sanctuary. Stumbling about in the darkness, he presented his offerings. When he tossed the incense into the fire, the flames shot upward, illuminating the chamber. The king beheld the sacred image of Huitzilopochtli. Then he saw the priest seated beside the idol, adorned in the skin of his daughter.

The eagle of the new land,
Tenochtitlán, perches on a cactus.

With a scream of horror, Achitometl ran from the temple. "Come, my followers!" he shouted. "They have killed and skinned my daughter! Death and destruction to these fiends and their vile customs. Let us slay them. Let us leave not a trace of them."

Out of [Copil's] heart sprouted the prickly pear cactus.

~ *Historia de las Indias de Nueva España*

Quickly the people of Culhuacan raised the alarm throughout their city. Hordes of armed warriors came running. The Mexica hastily grabbed their weapons and retreated toward the lake. Some of the men held off the attackers, while others lashed together their spears and shields. With the help of these crude rafts, the people crossed to the island in the middle of the water. Cold and wet, they spent the rest of the day huddled among the reeds and rushes.

That night, Huitzilopochtli heard the weeping of the women and children. Moved by their despair, he spoke to his priests. "Console the people," he said. "Tell them that they must endure their afflictions a little while longer. Soon, they will find their heart's desire."

The next day, the Mexica dried their clothes and cleaned their weapons. Then, they trudged on through the marshes, seeking the consolation their god had promised them. At last, they came upon a beautiful spring running with cool, clear water. Beside the spring stood an immense prickly pear cactus, sprouting from the heart of Copil. A giant eagle was perched among the thorns, with his wings stretched out toward the sun. In his talons, the eagle held a small bird with shining feathers.

The Mexica wept with joy at the fulfillment of the ancient **prophecy**. At long last they had reached the end of their journey. And when the eagle saw the people, he bowed his head in their direction.

So it was that Huitzilopochtli led his people, after many long trials and much traveling and bloodshed, to their new homeland. Upon these marches the Aztecs would build a great city and name it Tenochtitlán, "Place of the Prickly Pear Cactus." With courage and might, the Mexica people would go on to conquer all nations near and distant. Tenochtitlán would become a beautiful metropolis, the queen of all cities and the heart of the mighty Aztec Empire.

PART 2: Stories and Myths

# The Aztec World Ends

Hernán Cortés meets Moctezuma, the Aztec emperor.

While the Aztecs rose to be powerful warriors with a large empire spreading throughout the land, it was not to last. They were doomed to fall at the hands of mysterious foreigners. While they fought bravely, they could not protect themselves from the deadly plagues these strangers brought, and their myths led to confusion about who these strangers might be.

In April 1519, Hernán Cortés and an army of about six hundred conquistadors (conquerors) landed on the east coast of Mexico. Cortés had heard rumors of a splendid inland empire. Eager to get his hands on its treasures, he marched his forces toward Tenochtitlán. In a little more than two years, the Spaniards gained complete control of the magnificent Aztec capital and all its territories.

How could such a small army topple such a mighty empire? Early Spanish accounts gave the credit to Cortés's brilliant leadership and superior weapons. Modern-day historians point to a number of other significant factors. First, more than one hundred thousand warriors from tribes throughout Mesoamerica fought for the Spaniards, hoping to free themselves from Aztec domination. In addition, an epidemic of smallpox—a deadly disease brought by the Europeans—weakened or killed millions of people in and around Tenochtitlán. It is also possible that the Aztecs' religious beliefs contributed to their downfall. According to some accounts, the emperor Moctezuma may have believed that the strange, light-skinned foreigners were long-lost gods, returning as foretold in ancient prophecies. The Spaniards' behavior soon proved him wrong. By that time, however, the Aztecs had become too weak to overcome the invaders and their native allies.

Our retelling of the events surrounding the fall of the Aztec Empire is based on accounts written by the Aztecs themselves. Shortly after the surrender of Tenochtitlán, native survivors began to record their memories of the Spanish invasion in poems, chronicles, and plays. These sources offer a dramatic look at the history of the conquest from the viewpoint of the conquered. They also show us how the Aztecs drew on their ancient beliefs to explain the sudden catastrophic end of their world. In accounts blending history and mythology, the Aztec writers blame the conquest not only on Spanish armies, but also on spiritual forces set in motion at the very beginning of the world.

## The Omens of Destruction

Ten years before the arrival of the Spaniards, the people of Tenochtitlán began to see troubling signs of the terrors to come.

The first omen was a great flame that blazed in the night sky. It was shaped like a pyramid, with its base against the ground and its peak reaching up to touch the heavens. It seemed to bleed fire, drop by drop, as if the sky itself were wounded.

The second omen was the temple of Huitzilopochtli bursting into flames, though no one had set it afire. When the people threw water on the blaze, the tongues of flame leaped even higher. Thus, the home of the great warrior who vanquished the powers of darkness each morning was burned to ashes.

The third omen was a lightning bolt that struck the temple of Xiuhtecuhtli, oldest of all the gods. Only a light rain was falling, and there was no sound of thunder. The people said that the temple had been struck by a blow from the sun.

The fourth omen was a comet flashing across the sky in broad daylight. It raced from the place where the sun sets to the place where the sun rises, defying the natural order. The comet's three long tails showered sparks like red-hot coals, lighting the sky with their splendor.

The fifth omen was the wind lashing Lake Texcoco, the great body of water that surrounded and sustained the capital. The lake boiled with rage, foaming up to a

## Dramatis Personae

**Huitzilopochtli** (weet-see-lo-POACH-tlee) God of war and the sun; patron god of the Aztecs

**Xiuhtecuhtli** (she-wah-tay-KWAH-tlee) Ancient fire god

**Moctezuma** (mock-tuh-ZOO-muh) Aztec emperor; also known as Montezuma II

**Quetzalcoatl** (ket-sal-KO-wah-tul) God of the morning star

**Tezcatlipoca** (tez-kaht-lee-PO-kah) God of the night and darkness

**Hernán Cortés** (kor-TEZ) Spanish explorer and conqueror

great height. Then the waters dashed against the city, washing away half the houses.

The sixth omen was the voice of a woman weeping in the darkness. Night after night, she haunted the city, crying out mournfully, "O my beloved sons, we are lost! Where can I hide you?"

The seventh omen occurred when the men who fish in the lake snared a strange ash-colored bird, resembling a crane. On the crown of its head was a clear black mirror. The fishermen brought the wondrous bird to the emperor's palace. Moctezuma looked into the mirror and saw the night sky and all its stars. He looked a second time and saw a host of men, armed like warriors. They were approaching swiftly in well-ordered ranks, some walking, others riding on the backs of huge hornless deer. The vision filled the emperor with dread. He called for his magicians to explain it, but when they looked in the mirror, the image had disappeared.

The eighth and final omen was this: deformed men with two heads but only one body appeared in the streets of the city. The people brought the strange creatures to the palace. The moment Moctezuma beheld them, they vanished.

All these wonders filled the Aztecs' hearts with terror. The people wept and shouted, and the priests offered the hearts of many captives. Meanwhile, Moctezuma sat on his throne, brooding. The emperor knew that the world of the Fifth Sun was destined to perish, just like the four worlds before it. If the omens were signs that the end

A portrait of Moctezuma, the last Aztec king

was coming, there was nothing he or anyone else could do to prevent it.

## Tenochtitlán Falls

The sacred books tell us that long ago, Quetzalcoatl was forced into exile through the treachery of his brother Tezcatlipoca. The beloved god sailed away to the east on a raft made of serpents. But Quetzalcoatl made a promise before he left Mexico. He would return one day to vanquish Tezcatlipoca and reclaim his ancient kingdom.

So it was with great foreboding that the emperor Moctezuma heard the words of a messenger from a village to the east. "I saw towers or small mountains floating on the waves of the sea," the man reported. "The mountains bore a race of humans like none I have ever seen before. The men had long beards and yellow hair and skin as white as the flowers of the maguey."

This news distressed the emperor even more than the ten years of omens that had preceded it. It was the very year predicted for the return of Quetzalcoatl. Had the god crossed the sea with his divine attendants to overthrow the old order and reclaim his throne?

Moctezuma decided to dispatch messengers with gifts for the strangers, just in case they were gods. He ordered his craftsmen to fashion copies of the ancient raiment worn by Quetzalcoatl: a serpent mask made of turquoise, a necklace with a gold disk in the center, a jade bracelet with little gold bells, and a shield decorated with gold and mother-of-pearl and quetzal feathers. These treasures were packed in baskets, along with many other precious objects. Then the envoys journeyed to the coast, where they presented the emperor's gifts to Hernán Cortés, captain of the Spaniards.

When the messengers returned, they made their report to Moctezuma. They told him about the Spaniards' iron clothes and weapons. They described the thundering cannon that could shatter a tree into splinters and the tall creatures resembling deer, which carried the men wherever they wanted. Amazed and frightened, the emperor ordered his most gifted sorcerers to use their magic to send the mysterious strangers back to their own land. The magicians' spells failed completely. From then on, Moctezuma sat on his throne, paralyzed with fear and uncertainty. He did nothing but wait as Cortés and his army marched inland, slaughtering many people and making allies of others.

At length, the Spaniards reached the capital. The emperor himself went out to meet them. He did not resist when the men he had mistaken for gods took him prisoner in his own palace. He did not protest even when they seized his gold like hungry pigs gobbling up their supper. For many months, the greedy strangers ruled over the capital, using the captive emperor as their puppet. Finally, the Aztec warriors took up their spears and shields and cast out their captors. Moctezuma died in the fighting. Some say that he was put to death by the Spaniards; others that he was slain by his own people as a coward and traitor to his country.

For a brief time after the overthrow of the Spaniards, there was rejoicing in Tenochtitlán. Then, a

Moctezuma is captured by the Spaniards and pleads with the Aztecs to surrender.

terrible plague struck the city. The victims were wracked with coughs and covered from head to foot with agonizing sores. Many died before the disease released its grip on the people.

> [Moctezuma] went out to meet them … He showered gifts upon them.
>
> ~ *Florentine Codex*

While the city's defenses were weakened, the Spaniards returned with a new and even larger army. They surrounded Tenochtitlán with their warships and cannons. They destroyed the aqueduct that carried fresh water from the mainland. For eighty days, they held the capital under **siege**. The people were tormented with thirst and hunger. They ate lizards, corncobs, and salt grasses. Some chewed on deer hide. Some even ate dirt. No matter how weak they grew, the Aztec warriors still fought with courage each time the enemy raided the suffering city.

One night, a great flame appeared in the heavens, wheeling around like a whirlwind. It circled the city, then moved out over the middle of the lake, where it suddenly vanished. The weary people watched the omen in silence. The next day they surrendered. Cortés drove them out of Tenochtitlán, slaughtering some and making slaves of others. He stripped the city of all its treasures. Then he demolished the proud capital and built a Spanish city known as Mexico City on the ruins.

Temples and palaces lay in ruins, and the people were scattered. Even the gods seemed to have forsaken them, as the Spaniards condemned the sacred texts to be burned. The terrible omens that had predicted the Aztec downfall had been fulfilled. But Aztec people who had survived the fall of Tenochtitlán would record their stories and compose new books, recalling the spirit of the people and the glory of the empire. Their descendants kept the ancient traditions alive. Even today, there are those who believe that Quetzalcoatl will return one day, and the Aztecs will again live in glory.

## Songs of Sorrow

After the Spanish Conquest, Aztec writers lamented the destruction of Tenochtitlán. An unknown poet wrote the following song sometime around the late sixteenth century. The first verse refers to Tlatelolco, the once-great market district in Tenochtitlán where the Aztecs made a last stand against the Spaniards in August 1521. It is believed that as many as forty thousand Aztec men, women, and children were killed at Tlatelolco.

Nothing but flowers and songs of sorrow
are left in Mexico and Tlatelolco,
where once we saw warriors and wise men.

We know it is true
that we must perish,
for we are mortal men.
You, the Giver of Life,
you have ordained it.

We wander here and there
in our desolate poverty.
We are mortal men.
We have seen bloodshed and pain
where once we saw beauty and valor.

We are crushed to the ground;
we lie in ruins.
There is nothing but grief and suffering
in Mexico and Tlatelolco,
where once we saw beauty and valor.

# GLOSSARY

**Anahuac** The Aztec name for the Valley of Mexico; Anahuac (or Cemanahuac) means "Land between the Waters."

**city-states** Independent states, each made up of a city and its surrounding territory.

**codices** Early Aztec religious or historical texts consisting of pictographs (word pictures) painted on paper made from bark or deerskin, which were folded accordion style; the singular form is codex.

**deities** Gods, goddesses, and other divine beings.

**maize** A tall variety of corn native to the Americas.

**Mesoamerica** A part of Central America that was occupied by the Aztecs and other peoples in the days before European contact; Mesoamerica included most of modern-day Mexico, Guatemala, and Belize, as well as parts of Honduras, El Salvador, Nicaragua, and Costa Rica.

| | |
|---|---|
| **Mexica** | The people who migrated from the north and settled in the Valley of Mexico, founding the Aztec Empire. |
| **Mictlan** | The lowest level of the Aztec underworld. |
| **mythology** | The whole body of myths belonging to a people. |
| **myths** | Traditional stories about gods and other divine beings, which were developed by ancient cultures to explain the mysteries of the physical and spiritual worlds. |
| **Nahuatl** | The ancient language of the Mexica people, which became the dominant language of Mesoamerica; Nahuatl is still spoken in Mexico and many parts of Central America. |
| **patron** | A god or goddess that was believed to be the special protector of a group of people. |
| **prophecy** | A foretelling of something that will happen in the future. |
| **pulque** | An alcoholic beverage made from the fermented sap of the maguey plant, which was drunk or sacrificed as part of religious rituals. |

**quetzal** A Central American bird with bright green feathers.

**siege** A battle tactic in which an attacker surrounds a fortress or city, cutting off supplies to force the enemy to surrender.

**tzitzimime** Evil star demons that battle the sun at dawn and dusk and devour it completely during solar eclipses.

# AZTEC WRITING AND TEXTS

The Spanish conquerors of Mexico destroyed nearly all of the Aztec codices (texts consisting mainly of word pictures known as pictographs). Today, most of our written information about Aztec beliefs and mythology comes from books written shortly after the Conquest. These include traditional stories collected by Spanish chroniclers as well as new codices written by native people educated in Spanish colonial schools. Some of these post-Conquest texts were written in Spanish, others in Nahuatl, the ancient language of the Mexica people.

The myths retold in this book are based mainly on the following sources:

***Crónica Mexicana***
**("Mexican Chronicles")**

*Crónica Mexicana* was written around 1598 by Hernando Alvarado Tezozomoc, a grandson of the Aztec emperor Moctezuma. The text covers Aztec history from the late fourteenth century through the Spanish Conquest.

***Crónica Mexicayotl***
**("Chronicles in the Mexican Manner")**

Mythology and history overlap in these accounts of the origins of the Aztec people, the founding of Tenochtitlán, and other events through the Spanish

Conquest. The text was written in Nahuatl around 1609 by Hernando Alvarado Tezozomoc, the author of *Crónica Mexicana.*

### *Historia General de las Cosas de Nueva España* ("General History of the Things of New Spain"); also known as the *Florentine Codex*

Fray Bernardino de Sahagún was a Spanish missionary who came to Mexico in 1529. He spent much of the next twenty-five years interviewing Aztec elders about their traditional beliefs and myths. Native scribes recorded the interviews, and Sahagún edited those records to produce this encyclopedia of Aztec thought.

### *Historia de las Indias de Nueva España* ("History of the Indies of New Spain")

Diego Durán emigrated with his parents from Spain to Mexico around 1540. He later became a Dominican friar (a member of a Catholic religious order) and devoted his life to converting the Mexican people from their ancient faith to Christianity. His lengthy book on Aztec history and culture includes his Spanish translations of a now-lost Aztec history written in Nahuatl.

### *Historia de los Mexicanos por sus Pinturas* ("History of the Mexica Peoples as Told by Their Paintings")

This text on Aztec mythology was written by the Spanish priest and scholar Andrés de Olmos in the 1530s. It may have been based on a painted codex that has since been lost.

### *Histoyre du Mechique* ("History of the Mexicans")

A French scholar named André Thévet produced this translation of a now-lost sixteenth-century Spanish manuscript on Aztec mythology. The narrative includes the story of the goddess Tlaltecuhtli, whose body became the earth during the age of the Fifth Sun.

### *Leyenda de los Soles* ("Legend of the Suns")

This is the only surviving version of the Aztec creation story written in Nahuatl. It was produced by an unknown, Spanish-educated, Aztec author in 1558.

# FURTHER INFORMATION

## Books


Boone, Elizabeth Hill. *The Aztec World*. Washington, DC: Smithsonian Books, 1994.

Carrasco, David. *The Aztecs: A Very Short Introduction*. New York: Oxford University Press, 2012.

Coe, Michael D. and Rex Koontz. *Mexico: From the Olmecs to the Aztecs*. London: Thames and Hudson, 2013.

Dalal, Anita. *Myths of Pre-Columbian America*. Austin, TX: Raintree Steck-Vaughn, 2001.

Graulich, Michel. *Myths of Ancient Mexico*. Oklahoma: University of Oklahoma Press, 1997.

Jones, David M. *Mythology of the Aztecs and Maya*. London: Southwater, 2003.

León-Portilla, Miguel, ed. *The Broken Spears: The Aztec Account of the Conquest of Mexico*. Boston: Beacon Press, 1992.

Phillips, Charles and David M. Jones. *The Lost History of Aztec and Maya: The History, Legend, Myth and Culture of the Ancient Peoples of Mexico and Central America*. London: Southwater, 2014.

Schuman, Michael A. *Mayan and Aztec Mythology*. Berkeley Heights, NJ: Enslow, 2001.

West, David. *Graphic Mythology: Mesoamerican Myths*. New York: Rosen, 2006.

## Websites

**Anient History Encyclopedia**
www.ancient.eu/Tenochtitlán/

This site explores Tenochtitlán, the ancient Aztec capital, its mythological origins, and its historical importance. In addition to a map of the city during its peak and photos of reconstructed builds, the article is full of links to other relevant topics in Aztec culture.

**The Aztecs**
home.freeuk.net/elloughton13/aztecs.htm

This bright and colorful site was created by Derek Allen, former headmaster of Snaith Primary School in England. The site explores the Aztec world through stories, pictures, and interactive games. The text is available in both English and Spanish.

**Encyclopedia Mythica: Aztec Mythology**
www.pantheon.org/areas/mythology/americas/aztec

This online encyclopedia offers more than ninety brief articles on the Aztec gods and goddesses.

**Godchecker: The Gods of Aztec Mythology**
www.godchecker.com/pantheon/aztec-mythology.php

Godchecker is an online encyclopedia with a great sense of humor! The site includes a brief introduction to Aztec mythology plus lively articles on "a host of interesting Gods with completely unpronounceable names."

# SELECTED BIBLIOGRAPHY


Bierhorst, John, trans. *History and Mythology of the Aztecs: The Codex Chimalpopoca*. Tucson, AZ: University of Arizona Press, 1992.

Bierhorst, John, ed. *The Hungry Woman: Myths and Legends of the Aztecs*. New York: William Morrow, 1984.

Carrasco, Davíd. *Daily Life of the Aztecs: People of the Sun and Earth*. Westport, CT: Greenwood Press, 1998.

Carrasco, Davíd, and Eduardo Matos Moctezuma. *Moctezuma's Mexico: Visions of the Aztec World*. Niwot, CO: University Press of Colorado, 1992.

Caso, Alfonso. *The Aztecs: People of the Sun*. Translated by Lowell Dunham. Norman, OK: University of Oklahoma Press, 1958.

Durán, Diego. *The Aztecs: The History of the Indies of New Spain*. Translated by Doris Heyden and Fernando Horcasitas. New York: Orion Press, 1964.

Ferguson, Diana. *Tales of the Plumed Serpent: Aztec, Inca and Mayan Myths*. London: Collins and Brown, 2000.

León-Portilla, Miguel, ed. *The Broken Spears: The Aztec Account of the Conquest of Mexico*. Boston: Beacon Press, 1992.

León-Portilla, Miguel. *Pre-Columbian Literatures of Mexico*. Norman, OK: University of Oklahoma Press, 1969.

Markman, Roberta H., and Peter T. Markman. *The Flayed God: The Mesoamerican Mythological Tradition*. San Francisco: Harper San Francisco, 1992.

Phillips, Charles. *The Mythology of the Aztec and Maya.* London: Southwater, 2006.

Read, Kay Almere, and Jason J. González. *Handbook of Mesoamerican Mythology*. Santa Barbara, CA: ABC-CLIO, 2000.

Soustelle, Jacques. *Daily Life of the Aztecs*. Translated by Patrick O'Brian. Mineola, NY: Dover Press, 2002.

Taube, Karl. *Aztec and Maya Myths*. Austin, TX: University of Texas Press, 1993.

# QUOTATION CITATIONS

Quoted passages in sidebars come from the following sources:

"The Earth Monster," page 33, from the *Histoyre du Mechique*, in Roberta H. Markman and Peter T. Markman, *The Flayed God: The Mesoamerican Mythological Tradition* (San Francisco: Harper San Francisco, 1992).

"Two Sides of Everything," page 43, in Davíd Carrasco, *Daily Life of the Aztecs: People of the Sun and Earth* (Westport, CT: Greenwood Press, 1998).

"Rain Prayer," page 49, from the *Florentine Codex*, in Roberta H. Markman and Peter T. Markman, *The Flayed God: The Mesoamerican Mythological Tradition* (San Francisco: Harper San Francisco, 1992).

"Travelers in New Lands," page 67, from Miguel León-Portilla, Los Antiguos Mexicanos, in Davíd Carrasco and Eduardo Matos Moctezuma, *Moctezuma's Mexico: Visions of the Aztec World* (Niwot, CO: University Press of Colorado, 1992).

"Songs of Sorrow," page 83, from Cantares Mexicanos, in Miguel León-Portilla, *The Broken Spears* (Boston: Beacon Press, 1992).

# INDEX

Page numbers in **boldface** are illustrations. Entries in **boldface** are glossary terms.